D1551610

PARADE

Poems of Light and Dark Alike

FREDERICK BORSCH

ISBN: 0-9827584-0-5
Printed in the United States of America

Cathedral Center Press
An imprint of the Episcopal Diocese of Los Angeles
840 Echo Park Avenue
Los Angeles, CA 90026

www.ladiocese.org

Page design by Vicki Black
Cover design by Molly Ruttan-Moffat
Photo © mammuth/istockphoto.com

To Barbara

Each of these poems has its own life—an observation, a mood, a time—while there are also strands of narrative: growing up, wondering, love, prayer, children, ministry, loss, remembering, mortality, going on—life's parade.

CONTENTS

MORNING PRAYER

I am up this morning as your sun rises,
    return incredible again,
burgundy warming to gold on horizon's hearth.

I imagine other spectacles through myriad ages,
    in different shapes, colors and speeds,
on countless worlds of cold and fiery beauty,
    and I am out of mind.

Birds herald and call me back;
    their trees grow green, each its own shrine.

Crowned, you burst forth, emblazoning the sky
    before and beyond, reflecting all things,
and, though I think I know its dangers,
    I recognize my mothers and fathers
        come to worship you,
for, bathed in light, I, too, am on my knees
    and see beyond all times and worlds
        your shining here.

LOST AND FOUND

Granted a fairy's sleight of hand, why think
of something lost in a child's garden
where a quarter shines more than baby tooth
whose adult in the mirror peeks,
and in that photo I couldn't have cared less about,
beside a chum who also would be replaced
when we moved? So were the teachers,
with new schools, their songs and grades and, at last,
my spindly legs and arms with neat muscles
and hair gladly scalped
for summer fun.
Perhaps the best word would be cavalier
for all let go, new parts to explore.

"So fast," they said, he was growing. Too fast?
With so much to gain was something lost
when I began to wonder what they had found
that made me ask about my years.

LYRIC

A composing artistic
with the shaping of rhyme,
could be mere calculation,
and the counting of line;
but the throbbing of heart beat
beneath meter and form,
one can never dissemble,
nor contrive to seem warm.
So may striving poetic,
and now my metric feet,
come to tremble, to kindle
then to dance in life's heat:
this essay in lyric
become love's panegyric.

BITS

On waves in rippled space
spirit broods, spreading
the stellar ash, transformed
bursts into living
dazzled knots in the flow,
genetic wording
to spiraled paragraphs,
logos informing.
From those light years away,
whirlwinding and code,
suffering awareness
creation unfolds,
a semiotic world,
yet being told.

FABRICA

Both and either/or,
waves and/or particles,
matter is and is not,
fleeing in all directions,
still secret its articles
of that moment when
all may or may not
have been one, blown
in pulsing strings,
both chance and symmetry,
ruled indeterminacy,
to be known and unknown;
novae and holes,
gluons and quarks,
leaving their arcs,
ending in ways to be born;
"flaunting ... freedom from formula
they yet fabricate firm form."

THE PLAY

The ordered stage we were told to watch,
   with chance the outlaw actor,
    while now we see in every scene
the accidental factor.

Without random's role then stasis' rule
   would have creation frozen;
    as surely it's necessity
upholding all that's chosen

Not only once, but at every edge,
   as chaos threatens ever,
    bits link, shape life, they end and eat
where strange attractors gather.

There's tense interplay among the ways,
   in the flow to entropy,
    mere principles in subtle sets
gender vast complexity.

And in the joining, in the struggle,
   as the smarter, stronger form,
    in the suffering, in the learning,
perilous beauty is born.

BETTER BUGGED

In the telling of our lives
an ear still burns and rings,
self so fiercely struck
to deaden whining wings.

Pane jaggedly cuts a hole
where a book was to crush a fly;
fender bent or worse,
as though by a bee we'd die.

Might we with lives less annoyed,
whether by smiles or shrugs,
be better with our cares,
more graceful with our bugs.

AUGUST SIX

Taking with him Peter and James and John, he led them up a high mountain and was transfigured before them.	A-BOMB DROPPED ON JAPAN!

Up there horizon's edge might also be
the great water's shore, with the green river
draining this mountain and turning the plain
before generously making the sea.

Then on morning's wings the three of us
climb with him so far that another shore
is rising on that edge, and with it awe
there is no escaping, nor what we must.

Pray hand holds fast as the skies come open,
when for peace he looses day-star's secret,
falling without other benediction
than the radiance of night now given.

Who could have been known while yet in the womb
if not such humanity, face aglow
and clothes so dazzling white no earth's fuller
could possibly prepare them for this tomb?

Lit from within the columned cloud ascends,
majestic over us, hiding all presence,
though where does one go, if still at grave's bed
there also thunders "beloved" and sends

Terror on us and any loved dearly
by one for whom night and light could be like,
abandoning in the noonday darkness
his life offering said to be glory?

We may, of course, have been sleeping, a dream,
and it is time to come down from that edge.
The sun has returned, though it is cold now,
with silence only his death can redeem.

BURNING BUSH

Branches aglow, each leaf a flame,
perennial heat, never consumed,
crossed tree of life, crimson disclosing
its secret of birth in endless giving,
lures radiantly near,
eyes awed bright for fear
that such warmth diffuse
surety in entropy;
for there will be no touching
without dying and living.

AWAITING

In silence seemingly forever waits
the world's circling, moon rending, and cooling,
    for alchemy compounding to divide,
        and teem and dimly wait.

Word at last in the sand of promised land,
in river and rocks crafted through eons,
    for another coming home to expect
        birth, then last supper again.

The soul frets pretty paced and thirsting late
in lines to board, to fly, for baggage back,
    surfing the news in quiet longing
        for what alone it waits.

More gently pass the freckled fall, the turn
to ice and flowers again, inviting trust
    in gyring life, still hoping to its heart,
        for whom my soul would yearn.

HERE

Shining unseen through lavish space,
silent in darkness, until light
from light it comes over hills
and, inching down canyon walls,
engenders life, and then a word,
as though for mystery a place—
letting there be a world of sight
of its source illumining
a dimness now bright, words and song
shot through with sobbing, has us long
again, looking for the ray
in human heart and this womb's night.

FRED'S FLOOD

The other day a man I barely knew
said he'd sighted my blue canoe,
stored downside up—bow moored in a tree.
Smiling at my clergy collar, he asked
if I knew something he ought note,
whether he too should buy a boat?

I started to return his bandy
before a crafty vision stole my eyes,
for sometimes I do see river rising,
coursing white ribbed, then pooled and gliding,
down which we may escape.

I did not mean to bemuse his smile
by looking so far away,
but what was I to say?

CALIFORNIA HILLS

Great shoulders tan and
paler buttocks slumbering,
with verdant trails tangling
down golden flanks
to softer ravines,
fed by a dampness
of mysterious moistures,
secret of her sensuality,
our mother sleeps.

Pregnant from many invitations
to lie as naked born
in the shaded lap,
nosing the cool heat
and rhythms of her peace,
still she cannot tell
whether I will
with her morning wake.
This, too, she keeps.

FIRE CHILD

Some feel him not your child of fire,
through moist and fervid pangs of love,
hailed into the night world crying
in response to so much desire.

Yet how could you otherwise hear
the beating of his blood,
and taste the heat in every tear
that both your wounds would heal?

Until I touch the same bright wire,
in nerves by passion stroked to song,
and scent the warm and dripping wine,
will I too feel your child of fire.

TWINS

There was a rule
I learned in school
that three and one
are four and done.
With this rule at school I did not fool.

It did seem plain
that in the main
one should assume
so from the womb,
mainly the plain rule would be the same.

Yet we've said before,
on another score,
that by love's rod
all count is odd
and could well score more than four.

So we derive
from three to five
and praise the gifts
that logic shifts
in dividing to arrive at five.

This parable then
we'll say did happen
for future's sake,
without mistake,
how happened then our little men.

VERY MUCH

Hickory, dickory, Mother Goose,
Tommy Tonsey's come from France.
No more 'til you drink your orange juice.
Have we got any plastic pants?

Darling, I want you to know—
which one has started to cry?
As I started to say a moment ago,
They shook out their tails again fluffy and dry.

After you've washed the diapers, dear,
and built a garage for my friend, Noddy,
we'll find we have a few minutes clear
to make bottles and empty the potty.

Well, what I mean—Can you hear me?
Watch his bus! What a life!
No, I think he's bumped his knee
and cut off their tails with a carving knife.

Look, after they're all in bed—
Watch the bus! More eggs without fail,
and meat, soup, cheese and bread,
and, yes, *a black, swishy tail.*

Oh, they're dears, whom we cherish,
but I love—the laundry man, I guess—
you very much; so answer the door and
burp him, while I read *Tilly* and *Tess.*

FIRST RIDE

Nervy words of confidence and questions,
replaced now by twitchy silence,
watching my wrench
turn the nuts. I pull the bolts, and safety
of the training wheels falls away.

Cinch no longer, it will not stand
without a hand, I give to his,
watching the eyes,
as he holds mine in trust that I will let
him go, but not until he says,

and tries alone to make the wobbling straight,
crying not, and without laughter
should he falling—
hard on the skinning sidewalk or, we hope,
softer grass—need support again.

Calling for release, he yet lurches left,
then back into me heavily,
so sweet a weight
I could hang on, recalling my blue bike,
and with it my dad's strength and smell

late one afternoon, when I feel them both,
letting touch go, seeking balance,
as I do cry
and cheer us on when he begins to ride,
thinking perhaps he's on his own.

BUMP

Under the table legs grow longer
and, bumped by a foot now larger than my own,
clumsiness, sweet and hard, is known
in a hunger one fills no longer.

GOING, GOING

It's not that time goes so fast;
it never stops that makes things past.

STAR GAZING

I think of many like Odysseus,
with fixed eyes lifted on the sparkling throng,
glimpsing the heavenly hunter, here a bull,
and over there a bear, or wagon
with the dippers, big and small, lyre, lion,
then crab and crown, a unicorn, of course,
celestial zoo and living panoply
battling and turning the silent night, times
overlapping, transformed in other eyes,
as with pharaoh, hippo and crocodile,
while still and strewn above come together,
constellations signaling some design
worthy of our story, our fear and song,
their names, Orion, Sagittarius,
our lives enlarging, perhaps directing.

So what is it with me? I have the maps
they drew, bright dots to dots of our dark sky.
Is it faith that can't connect, now knowing
how hundred light years, they tell, are between
those neighbor lamps, sky so full and empty
with no plan? or just enchantment lacking
as I gaze in awe but without story?
Tipped dippers I can trace, a studded belt,
north star, but little more.

LETTING GO

Of course, there comes a time
(though who can know how quick that course?)
when, trying to console,
only clichés come home,
together echoing
with memories and our footsteps,
through the rooms searching
for boy-men flown.

"It was only yesterday!"
"Don't look away,"they said.
"They'll grow so fast."
And so they did.

But how do you know
how mixed the pride and loss
of role will be, and the surprise
at one's own change now?

"You wouldn't want them
    not to grow,
would you?" No.
"Hold them very close;
    then let them go."
But who could know?

"Of course, they are ready
and not ready";
yet not to go
means never ready.

How do you prepare,
after caring so fiercely
to let go with the freedom
you prepared so carefully?

"They were always a gift,
to be loved with open arms,
a temporary trusteeship.
You knew its terms."

"If you love them more
    themselves
and less yourself in them,
it may be easier then
not to want them homesick."

"They'll keep coming home."
"The balls, the beds, the books,
are still theirs."
Yet different look.

And so there in the fall,
standing in that hall, turning we meet,
years later, different together, knowing
there is more for each other,
more time for self and lover,
and we discover gratitude
and accomplishment
as, arm in arm, we relent.

NAUGHT MUSIC

To make a poem or listen to it
one must have overheard
the silence of the spaces,
quiet between each word.

Without a naught the ones could not
be hundred one or tens,
nor ever on computers run
our many computations.

For Wolfgang, Bartok, Beethoven,
And all of their musicians,
no melody is without rests
in myriad instrumentations.

It's stories' gaps that let run free
our imagination,
while hollowness by crafty Moore
creates configuration.

Amid the atoms and the suns
there's also nothingness,
places left for something else
we once called emptiness.

Nullity, it now turns out,
is void with potency,
lacunae filled with what may be
and dark with radiancy.

From silence in such darkness,
and cause for life to long,
out of all the none there is
comes here a breath and song.

HALL OF FAME TRIP

The judge had Mountain for a middle name:
that I remembered, and a pillar, I was told,
with those cold and righteous eyes, of rectitude
and integrity. There'd be no scandal
on his watch, no black in baseball.
He cleaned the game and made our Sox white again.

"We never made it back for years," dad wept.
You should have seen old shoeless Joe.
"Say it ain't so," they begged of him,
but he had helped fix those games
with Chick and Swede; they brought such shame.
He scrubbed all that and kept us clean for years.

In the year Judge Landis died a negro
in an army bus would not sit back
for being black. I saw them both in the Hall
where the same glint stares toward right
both knowing there would be a fight
'Ere Mr. Rickey got his victory.

He'd had to steal from first with all the blame,
as on the field they'd throw black cats
with cat calls of hate and fear,
'til Pee Wee draped his arm at last
and could come Monty, Satch, and from their past
Buck and Josh in whose hand the ball looks white.

GRAND CANYON

Storied sand and life,
five thousand years by inches,
pressed, uplifted, billionaire,
more lost than saved
in temples sculpted without myth
of vastly vaulted treasure.

Here a mute shard, saga
fallen down the layered eras,
smoothed by this muddy geologist
from a hundred peaks away,
rushing unhurriedly to draft new tales
of ancient marine.

Still warm from but one sun,
I behold with infant eyes,
now drawn the walled aisle,
past half of earth, in slice of stars,
some this night shining
before a canyon day.

A grain of time and space,
here to see and guess,
not only thinking
but to think of thinking
on all that seems beyond
awed reverence and thanksgiving.

LAYERS

All grave stones in different times,
tomb, tumulus, temple and türbe,
monuments and mausoleums, stelae,
engraved at times or in time erased,
built in or upon another faith
in savior, healer, sage,
Christ, Prophet and Cybele,
their forts, their homes, a trafficked city.

Heads and glorious bodies,
soldier, wife, emperor, athlete,
frozen in courtyards and museum,
once pearled eyes now sleepless,
an arm, nose, penis lost in some fall,
yet more appealing our humanity.

Whole towns, too, houses and law,
sports, baths, latrines and library,
half columned street,
theater set still for its players,
work, worship, carved, etched and weathered,
marble, wrack and rock
again upraised by plan and art, then ruined.

Violence is also enshrined in their arms
(all crusaders in one cause or another,
and greedy, even lovers of the stones),
with earthquakes heaving up the quarry,
then fearfully shaken down,
as though in some larger struggle,
to see if all may be leveled.

BETWEEN

What so distinctively is shared
may be kept *entre nous,*
sliding mid two and one;
or, say, red and a green,
linked and divided together;
or the distance from here to there,
leaving little or much as the mean,
set in ready to go with time's imprecision,
parenthesis, adverb, life's preposition,
meting out sickness and health, richer and poorer,
our work and our rest, for self and for other,
mid longing and fears, day and/or night,
the cutting of cords, silver, umbilical,
while providing the pairing
that joins and sets all apart,
ours to apportion, now and not yet,
to be held and halved, just between us.

SWIFTLY

Green and gold on pinion tips,
balanced as though motionless,
hovering for its head to be still,
that from this fragile a flower,
on earth circling per hour,
so slender of tongues might find drink.

Through my window I'm watching,
tiny bird, dark and dawning
from beginning that we may have place,
and along, too, for the ride
might find them as guide
for this cadence here to be holding,
and with their spirit's poised pace
fly our swiftness to grace.

PONIES

From somewhere my picture was taken,
tight smiling in hope I'll be found.
I'm riding for dear life a pony,
while merrily we go round and round.

Bigger ponies made me feel older,
higher up the pole, up and down.
My child, how I've worked to be up there,
while merrily we go round and round.

I climb on a horse yet more gilded,
hurdy-gurdy churns out gay sound.
My dear, now I'd like just to sit here,
while merrily we go round and round.

AROUND

I would say this of that;
that is, that all goes round;
hush, my child, years and planets,
eons wound, if wounded,

an orbed universe,
its ringing spheres and disks,
here cycling seasons for sowing,
then reaping, our dancing and mourning

in iris, pupil, too, balled
for observing or not,
what might be said or held
with half an eye to a torn veil.

Hush child, though grown now
you may but go round
the endless endings,
your metaphors to sound around.

OR

First some twigs, dry and crackling
as we could find, a crumpled nest,
then finger-size in tepee type
with thicker for an outer frame or,
on wind or wood or whim depending,
log cabin is another form, fun
to stack the little pyre,
and with cupped match and blowing softly
teach my children,
and they'll teach theirs,
more ways than one to start our fire.

SOUL NIGHT

Darkness shivers the soul,
huddling before embers,
clutched in thinning vestments,
whispers on what one remembers,

of when each shadow was the play
with light upon the hills,
clouds of unknowing incense,
doubts intrigue of riddles.

Forced now by these night watches,
was not that game the dream?
a romancing of the day,
of what then could be seen?

I sip from the cold spirit;
I have been here before,
which warms lingering hope
that yet there can be more.

Surely the hills will return,
first as ghostly sentinels,
grey, then rose and green,
bearing all life's potential,

and all its heartbreak, too—
roots and leaves, graves and seeds,
passion, pageantry, love's death
beyond all word of creeds.

In a gyre my faith is turned,
perhaps at dawn believing,
darkness not to be foe,
rather the way of leaving

that which is not faith
in the one who has both made,
toward whose vision aspiring
the cycling may yet be laid.

Not just forever round then,
but rising some spiral arc,
toward the Omega for whom
alike are both light and dark.

REFLECTION

His had to be the more surprise,
for I had expected I might glimpse him,
at least a reflection in that other land,
where summers ago we made life and
pleasured without much looking back or forth.
By the pool I saw something in his eyes.

Perhaps not quite, for his glance drifted then,
and I could not be sure that he was I,
was scared to stare, that he might recognize
who would be and not, and jeopardize
a fragile ripple, where my memory
warped with his imagination ran,

Which may tell us why neither with words tries,
daring wisdom, child-father-son, to share,
and finally I half-turned as if to end,
when I thought I caught, in that mirror bent,
him look up again. Yet, if I cannot recall,
is it memory or imagining lies?

Or both? for so blurring, blurred can
memory be, while neither are we sure
if any thought, back or forth, can comprise
much more for us than fiction's guise,
though even that relies on some membrane,
frail link between what is and now has been.

So still I wonder who he was, the Is
I've been and am, if they ever meet,
while he, I guess, reflects on who I am
and he will be, in another land, and
how he is in me and I in him, now
may recall when I saw something in my eyes.

COURSE

Wind-riding storm upon storm,
swirling hills and rising rivers,
changing but little weathers,
until one sun-slanted morn,
when I hear the waters course,
rushing to meet their source.

And then clouds giving way,
so soon the streams flow quiet,
for the grass too harsh the light
that soft emerald days might stay;
sun hard now, taut and arching,
even memory parching.

There seems so slight a season,
sparse time for finding balance,
space for any stance
to ask about some reason,
before flowers fill their course
and we must return our source.

How much hope then, if at all,
might we take from earth beginning
its headless, endless cycling
before once more it is fall?
In this might be traced a course
that yet gestures toward some source?

RECALL

Closed eyed, each about me I try to keep
in a child's game, how on a tray all
might by the winner be saved, though I know
much from this room will finally fall.

Perhaps better to try for just a few,
as I see, now down the hall,
how each time it's longer, more rooms, of course,
some smaller than I recall,
often out of every order,
more sparsely furnished, a darkened wall.

It may be but by a curtain parting
that sun on this table does fall;
and in this a little light my telling
how this room joins that hall.

KEYS

Nearly at the drawer's back, odd foreign coins,
old cufflinks and, without its ring, this key
I recognize, an extra somehow kept,
perhaps to recall how the door opens
on the pine planked floor, with its polish scent
and laughter up the stairs. I could have wept
for pressing it so hard against my palm,
as if so doing might remind me more.

With a former watch there lies another
that now will not unlock. I guess office
left behind? Or some inner door I've shut.
And then the wagon's key with which we start,
kids tucked in back, and to the shore we'd drive.
Once it hauled home a Christmas tree we'd cut,
then carried up the porch, as I with this
feel that turning and closing of our door.

RETURN TO TADOUSSAC

La baie, la plage et le village,
extraordinaire how deep infold,
in banks that seemed beyond reprieve,
years past, perdu to be retold:
the pastels of the evening's light,
berries' savor and then horn's sound,
the words français, this chair, a cup,
the crack in closet door are found
here cool and clear, so hidden well
that their retrieve is effortless,
causing mind on mind to wonder
and to imagine, try and guess
how much more of la vie encode
could be awaiting such download.

REUNION

Apple and elm down.
one pruned limb by limb,
the elm split crashing lawnward
one wild, sky-flashing night.

Through time the green gray pine
has spread so many layers
that one would need be small again
to see its old top through the window.

With hometown friends I'm met,
to contemplate at once
these years in story telling,
of stumps and new branches.

LOGAN AIRPORT

"World 30 going over the end"

The sodden clouds at last releasing
    to the comforting lights, our earth,
with wheels now lowered, flaps extending,
    inner rhythms lifting too,
for there the dotted lamps and sheening
    blackened ice and crusted snow,
as all is straining, heavy hanging,
    hard and hurled on frozen track,
with sound as much as light now streaming,
    waiting for the thrusting back
against the slipping tonnage hurtling
    by the turnings fleeting past;
no voice at all, all caught alarming
    that we cannot seem to slow,
so little time to fear the crashing
    and live burning we might die;
one word of prayer, loved faces lurching,
    yours and boys in terror's night,
as rattling fiercer and careening,
    swerving from electric bridge,
down goes my head as we are splashing,
    up then stunning, breaking plane,
with heart and breath so near to stopping,
    out of darkness still there's sight,
and in the waters yet this roaring
    over shouting we're all right.

FATHER DEATH

Collapsing catastrophically, a brilliance
once lighting life around,
now exhaust, unable to sustain
all it has been, cannot prevent
        fearful end.

Struggling, the breath that urged
my life curdles helpless
in antiseptic morning gloom;
yearning with last passion it tries,
        then still dies.

Utterless dark, silence beyond
being seen or seeing,
outside all laws of space or time,
Darth Vader screwing every coal
        in his black hole.

Ending rivers dueling with light
through trees, or hope of sunrise
warming cold eyes, or books or birds,
lost just the whisper of prayers,
        even stars,

lovely lights, I once was told
to think of them in velvet sky,
my loved ones, but now at night
I fear last memories sucked dry
        in that hole die.

Singularity, they call the unfelt heart
of the annihilating hell mass,
so dense that nothing forever escapes,
in which all that was our days
            ends all ways.

And then some space-struck physicist,
no better than astrologist, crueler
than mystic prophet, leaps far
beyond our way of knowing,
            speculating

that what disappears into that grave,
beneath all law and reason, unknown
as either energy or matter, might by miracle
be transformed to new universe,
            and the verse

I want to hear claims for you
that dark and light are both alike,
out of nothing and never beyond
more than universal love, they and we
            with you may be.

STURGEON NARROWS

Not only twice, young man and older now,
but more than forty years I've fished this stream,
swum it cold and fathomed pools and currents,
not all summers, but enough to have seen
a brown bear when we surprised each other
as she swiped fish among the rocks just where
the waters shallow clear and rush so well
that only strong arms can come cross it here.

Those friends and wife and sons have paddled with
and against the steady, moving river.
We have drunk and fed from it, while hearing
its ongoing passage with each other.

Another time alone above its draw
I lured a pike whose instinct knew the stream
a place to tug the canoe in again
and again, 'til I caught him tired and clean.

Although a birch has fallen in the bend,
it looks unchanged, the river stepped into
first those years ago, having read time's truth:
this is other water, each time anew.

Stepping again, I feel the cold, but sense
as well water flowing age upon age,
here and there, for all others gone, to come,
what yet goes on among enduring change.
I see the bear and feel the pulling pike,
looking up and down the river, its same
shaped flux, forever changing, cold and bright,
as this foot has its place within the stream.

DIFFERENT

Almost too excited we can get,
waiting for his "ready, set"
and then "go, go, go," which is why
I take so many sips and must try
then to keep mouth dry, to wipe it dry
and never let it be too wet and may
use my shirt, Coach says, "O.K."
when it's our olympic day,
and it's hard not to tug up and down
on it or make the sound
to "go, go" and jump up and down
before we hear him say and can keep
my eyes straight and leap and leap
ahead, and also with my arms keep
swinging back and forth,
keep them swinging back and forth,
but still staying on the course
in our special meet because
Coach says we're special for what each one does
and also my Dad says because
we're different and loves me
because of that and likes to see
how fast that I can be,
and, I think, also because when
Stevie stumbles and Maya trips on him,
we all race back to get our friend
and help each one out
and help them up and shout
"go, go" so we can all about
run fast again and each one win.

DAM

Sun Yat-sen, for heavens' sake,
even invading Japanese,
then Chiang's Koumintang,
with help from our Bureau (I love this)
of Reclamation, and, no doubt, Madame Chiang,
so idolized by those conservative,
for, my friends, we're talking real consensus here,
as Mao also wrote a poem:
"sun, sky and stream";
it was his idea and he swam it,
the Yangtzee, Chou and Jiang behind him,
and when you stop to think, our Hoover, too,
poor guy for the economy,
but not cheap electricity, and FDR,
for there was as well Grand Coulee,
good fortune to sound so like
the workers, their sacrifices
at so small a cost, lives and fish,
thousands here now there, three gorges full,
checking floods downstream at least,
they think; oh, some silting, a few species,
billions for old towns and folks moved,
so new, so add your name, too,
for less oil burnt, we'll pray, and,
my brothers and sisters all, feel the swell.

WOMAN BISHOP BLACK

Drawn from slavery, oppressions' child,
still the malign of color's poverty
and gender's bar to equality,
around her hung,
with her own prophetic words
as though in calumny.

She cannot be, not be allowed,
not possible, her gender most,
but surreptitiously her race
with those cadenced cries
for all others, within and out
this supposed genteel house,
bringing refusals, even to know her,
especially her.

Yet now from her knees she rises, called of God
from among those last made first,
one among disciples. Adorned,
her words are mitred flames
on female brow, and in her hand
a staff to protect and bring home,
color and womanhood all clothed,
she stands, she turns,
and is, with all hers before and after,
as with her God all things possible,
now, for us, apostle.

MARILYN

It's a story that might be told
with many players, sometimes old,
but young ones, too, and fiercely sure
that Randall was not right or pure
and could not be ordained a priest,
nor Hong enough of ours, at least,
that he should minister at Grace,
though maybe in another place.
There then, however, came a day
when like that injured man they lay
beside the road, all hurt and scared,
and who but Hong or Randall dared
to stop and share rare sacraments
of mercy's wine and oil's emollients.

In this case, full of smiles, a man
told me for women priests his ban.
To his bishop he'd show respect,
nor would he join another sect;
yet his creed would never falter,
his insistence that the altar
was surely best for men reserved
where only in the past they'd served.

A year or two went by before
he told me he had not forswore
his opposition firm and strong
that he had meant to be lifelong,
though when a sister dear to him
fell gravely ill in far off state,
and he had gone with her to wait
for healing and for hope again,
it was, at first to his chagrin,
a woman priest who prayed with them
and brought such love he'd said "amen"
and stretched his hand to take the bread,
and one thing to another led.

So now he wanted me to know
that women priests were still so-so.
He would continue with his doubt,
denying this a turnabout;
he might confirm his ban again,
except, that is, for Marilyn.

CROSSING

It was another fifty second mile
before I tried to smile away the foolishness,
glad I saw alone, though
sorry, too, not to have someone
with whom to share the turtle staggering
cross the road, trucks behind us;
for I had thought of stopping, imagined
slamming brakes and swerving the graveled shoulder,
somehow then to slip among the tonnage
and rescue what so rarely
in this world can be saved.

Maybe she just did crawl over,
neighbors dodging as best they could,
so that in the dun ditch squeezed out
those bits of life that drove her cross,
though I have been so often wise enough
to pass by, hurried, or had to,
that a dead mess won't leave my Samaritan alone,
as I let two more Stuckeys by
before I settle for restroom and a coke
and whatever prayer this is that
in this world might be saved.

ON THE PLANE

Sleek and lordly looking
above the puffed coasters, their shadowed faces
draped on trees and hills,
belying speed, cross roads and homes,
going to important places,
I cannot see into your world,
you, wrapped so minutely in spaciousness.

Then, in ordinary scale, late that day,
I, for a moment, shade my eyes
to see your speck sketching its contrail,
thinning now and fading.

FREE AT LAST

At the Prague Zoo, the waters drowned a gorilla in its cage and forced keepers to put down an elephant and a hippopotamus they were unable to rescue. A seal escaped.

—*Los Angeles Times*, August 15, 2002

A nice life, it may seem to you:
no need to hunt our food or fight for sex,
while safe from those who could attack,
even a sweet-talking veterinarian,
her pills and shots,
and all the others fenced away,
holding up their little ones and pointing.
But we were not made for this, and
while, yes, the moving water terrified,
it was still more like home to us,
especially one you call a river horse.

I was excited to think of trying
out the Vltava. I might have
escaped, too, floating as we do so well,
and maybe found a bar downstream
and ordered my own drink and things to chew,
though who knows for sure what escape
means for sister seal in a peopled world.

The roar you heard was my laughter
to see her slither off, and a rising hope,
for I never saw the gun until
your fear of me free, huge and strong,
you said to be a kind of kindness
to put me down.

IN THE CAR

I went alone for Sydney's ashes
to the same vet where we would go before,
giddy to be riding in the car
until he saw that door,
and big dog that he was —
so blustery with squirrels and other dogs —
began to fret and tremble
when it was at most a shot.
Yet perhaps deep down he knew more,
perhaps we all do,
certainly within himself something more
when she first suggested arthritis,
before the morning he could not stand
and had to be carried there.
A few days earlier, I see him so eager
for his walk, yet for his frisbee leaping,
giving what may only be called a smile
as he nearly doubled back upon himself,
scuffling forward and looking round,
shepherding us when he could.

I thought I was over it.
Pets do die, however much we talk to them,
while there seems all that mutual care.
It was several months before I got round to it,
between the grocery and the cleaners.
I just sat him on the seat next to me
and cried.

POINTS

I have made my points so many times
I wonder how they could be missed,
    more, my whole argument dismissed
    in their asking what my main point was.

At times I've tried so many points,
pattern perhaps or scatter shot,
    on other days midpoint forgot
    what point I'd meant to sharpen up.

On occasion, I do realize,
someone a finer point has made,
    mine given then a lower grade,
    and on some score even, I guess, lost.

So that, well they might be asking now,
whether there is point to this,
    whether I again will miss
    all that has been pointed out.

For I'm not holding it all pointless,
but I know it is my worry
    that even after all this hurry
    I'm, in some way, way behind in points.

HOW DARING

Who do you think you are,
showing up in the church of the three year old?
How dare you be here wordless
before a father's hollow eyes?
How dare you in the faint cologne even touch
the mother's mother, agonizing for her child,
dressing the brothers in their white shirts,
trying to open some hymn of goodness,
while sadly wondering had you shown up then,
whether their brother would have died?
Poor Darwin's chaplain goes about blindly
fingering every hole in the congregation,
and the odor is everywhere.
Sobbing like you do,
you dare show up again.

SEASONS

Perhaps love, but first more admiration,
a kind of awe that you'd already been,
and I could fit beneath your shade and stand
on your gnarled feet and hoist myself and feel
the whisper of your loft and what you'd seen.

Then together through the seasons,
our snow caught on your arms, and every spring
my mild joy, too, while at least some falls
I have swept your stiff and fragile offering,
and wept the beauty of your barrenness.

I've watched you taste the sun and sensed your roots
thirsting to the pond, making yourself home
for quarreling squirrels, and standing in this
for life ongoing and for all I've known,
all that is here for me on each return.

The change first seemed so slight I rubbed my eyes
because, I saw, you looked enough unchanged
I could now imagine your still standing
with myself gone. And you appeared aloof,
or at least with the caring somehow changed.

ONE AT A TIME

One leg at a time they put on their pants;
presidents, professors, ballplayers do it
   in brown pants, blue pants,
      short pants with underpants.

Ladies, gentlemen engage in the dance,
tilting, leaning, almost jumping they do it;
   one leg at a time they pull on their pants.

Blue jeans and trousers, boxers and panty pants,
fancy and poor folk; it's hard to avoid it
   in brown pants, blue pants,
      short pants with underpants,

Younger and older may vary the stance,
but the large and tall, quite skinny: all do it;
   one leg at a time they put on their pants.

At times in their wiggles you'd think they had ants;
While most prefer standing, a few'd rather sit
   in brown pants, blue pants,
      short pants with underpants.

Life can be challenging just to keep balance;
presidents, poets and firefighters do it;
   one leg at a time they put on their pants
      in brown pants, blue pants,
         short pants with underpants.

GOING ON

One day tricky Dick, then old Frankie boy,
and, of course, there was dad, and down the street
that sweet gal I but gabbed with now and then,
followed by grit and grin Burt Lancaster,
which makes me, for some reason, think of Kate
"God Bless America," and on the steps
of our Abraham, no less, "My Country
'Tis of Thee," sung so proud and hauntingly.
Bless Marian Anderson, and Satch Paige
who knew you sometimes win and sometimes lose,
while on other days you just gets rained out.

I knew them all, at least it seemed I did;
that includes the three kids mashed from life
in the head-on crash on route forty-five.
I saw it on the news a while ago,
with all of those who went down on that plane.
Before them Cesar Chavez and the guy
who sold me vegetables and my paper,
whose way of looking down and up at you
reminded me of my science teacher,
who must be gone. And the amazing thing
is that any of us are still around;
I mean we all die, but it's if and when
one tries to think on it, I realize,
it's because we are going one by one,
or in little clumps that living seems not
to notice or change that much, managing
to go on, which is good, and somehow strange.

POST PATTERN

Praise fields, soft and damp, and so springing green
to older legs that they begin to jog
and think again of cleats cutting left and hard,
with safety now behind and running free,
as overhead the pass just off my right,
in turning that is all I care to see;
and, with heart stretching out to gather in,
I tumble down into the sweetest earth.

PARADE

"I want to see, I want to see,"
my little grandson pulls on me.
I lift Jack up that he may point
to firemen smiling from their truck,
hooting when they whoop its horn.
Next horses and a marching band,
and, by God, an elephant thumps ahead
of open cars and pretty girls, I notice,
waving to a squad of cyclists,
black and red and white and blue
in the parade that's passing through.

It's then I see I want to see
new poets, next musicians, scouts,
explorers of the quarks and stars,
even global warming, if more caring,
undoing of some old diseases:
all he may see this century,
seeing he cannot shoulder me.

STORM

There were gusts at first, a kind of huffing.
Coming from the east it might've blown past,
but soon the waves darkened, and lashing about
and around our slight craft, began washing
over the gunwales and pitching the mast,
wearing us out in heart-wrenching dips and swaths.

And there, lofting his gaping mouth again,
was that beast, Leviathan, the monster
from the depths of all our fears, made for sport,
you say, but for us terror-struck the end
would come, while astern whom we call master
slept, his legs athwart, on that damn cushion of his.

He rests, while we like drunken sailors lurch
and in panic sicken it is chaos
that triumphs over all our good and games,
of chance and the hoping on in the search
through many maybes for what's not lost
with all our names to the grim and grinning one.

Bailing madly, at it and him we shout,
"Don't you care that we perish? Rouse yourself,
if you are he who you say you are — Lord!"
who now, rising up to face our doubt,
with his word commands both sea and wind well
and, all restored, asks what other fears he might spell.

OVER TIME

I'd like to think I've care for you
and the world in which you live,
its water, winds and trees, schools,
new museums, music that give
you your enjoyment, love and hope
beyond all my knowing,
in another century unborn.
It's now of you I'm thinking as
in common hand you kindly hold
a splice of progeny,
and in your time imagine
this bit of ancestry.

For you, though, it is easier,
as for me for Booker T.,
Florence Nightingale, Old Abe,
even love lost Marc Antony,
so different, yet I know their names
and something of their colors,
hair and skin, their songs and food,
their suffering with their lovers,
that I can see and conspire with them,
as you may with me, but I —
because of time's one door
toward you can barely more than pry
with this imagined empathy,
and say how unfair it seems
you are so impersonal
in the way our light must stream.

Yes, I do read science fiction,
though that is, of course, the deal;
while you know I must have been,
in my book you're not yet real,
so hard to share a world with,
a common humanity,
while still it will yet be so,
mine, then your mortality.

And if all this seems presumptive
to you stuck in this stream, too,
I'll also forge forgiveness,
hoping you'll think I've care for you.

POET'S PRAYER

Love appears as word,
a way our speech,
of an inner grace unseen,
may be signifier.

Hope might find better metaphor,
allusive, something saying
is not, yet perhaps something
in Light, Shield, or Mother Love,
Father, Son, Spirit, Life Itself, Fire.

Pen in hand I'd kneel again
for Goodness, Wisdom, Beauty,
though still in this chair finding God
a higher figure rustling in prayers
that, if only for our sake, I ask
you would inspire.

CLOSING PRAYER

Some lingering of prayer or song,
ending sound in a darkening church,
a scrap of scripture: for God alone
my soul awaits, my soul does thirst.

In the last stains of blues and green
I hold still the book and bare scent
of candles' snuff, awaiting, too, my prayer
of soul alone in longing bent.

SCARS

I think I understand
how by combustion long, or swift and bright
the eyes and ears, my legs, hands, arms, each gland,
then even teeth, bone at last, from all sight
are gone to dust and sand.

Hard although to think
of being not, and of these my fingers,
which now move and write, and every link,
perhaps saving this, whereby one lingers
with you, to gravely sink.

In faith one thinks, one hopes
of that other tent, of some reclothing,
that not in nakedness, but with new tropes
of sight and voice, and ourselves emerging,
all dressed in shining coats.

Yet still I think, would know
what happens to the scars I feel, I've earned:
the door, then shovel crossed on a child's brow;
more by sport and in a paned glass door turned
by a little girl, oh!

So I think of mother,
phone again ringing, nearly once a year,
some cut, or fracture when for her brother
sister shouting, he fell so far, so near
to breaking heart of her.

As I think, too, of scars
engraved on the bone of leg and arm,

how a cheekbone cracking in a fight mars
now not at all (I laugh), nor the nose harmed.
All past now, all honors.

I think how it went on:
of one of these fingers jaggedly snared,
and finer lines of healing incision,
gall bladder gone, back, shoulder, lung repaired.
Yes! quite a collection!

They must, I think, stand, too,
for colder wounds, acts that seemed unfeeling,
undone and done, sharp words, as most I rue,
my cuts to others, for whose scars healing,
too, I will pray anew.

Not least I think of times
trying, trying to hunger and vying
for some modicum of fairness, those signs
for others, of just hands, a heart sharing,
caring against our crimes.

Which has me think of night
long wrestling with the one not letting go,
who for some yet veiling love and its rite
of wounds that may heal sends me limping so
into the breaking light.

Then I can but think well
of holes hammered in palms and feet, his side,
and, why not, too? as saw slipped or chisel
when like us learning, so that when he died,
they after knew love still.

I think some way they're laid
in days to come, if not on our new selves,
then in that life with whom as we are made
hurts, known and knelled, are so reformed it tells
that they with we are saved.

AS WELL

Of course we die alone,
marked by loss and brokenhearted,
even doctors say so,
and eternity seems vast,
while there is love, as well, my gratitude,
and where go these unless you—
as I am parted?